CW00502701

Stop Losing:
Master the Art of Self
Awareness and
Mindfulness

ANTHONY ODLE

ISBN: 9781711200583

To my Wife,

To the one who sees the King within, to the most powerfully gentle. To the answer to my fervent prayers. To the one who has built so effectively with me from day one Sept 5th, 1994. To the one who is who I am. To the love that strengthens me. To the peace that comes from being in your presence. To the joy that never leaves. To the hope that I see in the eyes of the children. To the power that comes from God. To the memories that we have created on purpose, to the plans that we have for the future. To the things that will come, good and bad. I know that together we win!

Love you more and more with each breath,
Latoya my Queen, my Love, my Friend, My Why.

To my amazing kids,
Khiera, Jaiden, Nia, Terae & Kaela
DREAM | CREATE | LIVE

Table of Contents

Introduction

We all want to win, well at least I do. In order to get to that point of victory, we need to understand exactly what it is we want whilst appreciating what we don't want. I could have easily entitled this book Start Winning or something along those lines and yet that was never the aim. For those who have lost at anything, it can be hard to come to terms with. We can plan and prepare, strategize and evaluate and still lose.

What I have observed is that we often have habits and rituals that are so deeply ingrained and that stretch back so far that we accept that they are as much a part of us as the color of our eyes. What if this were open for negotiation? What if through a series of simple tasks we could reframe our world, our actions, our future? In this book, I invite you on a journey where you look yourself squarely in the eyes and ask yourself "Who taught you that?"

Self-awareness is about knowing who you are. It is the ability to define yourself in terms of the way you think, the way you feel, your wants, your needs, your values, your personal beliefs, your strengths, your weaknesses, your expectations, and your aspirations. In a sense, self-awareness is about understanding just how unique you are, and how your uniqueness adds value to the world, as you continually grow and change.

Self-awareness is critical in how you view the world and its opportunities. The quality of the life you lead is determined almost entirely by your perspective. We consciously and unconsciously judge every experience we have against our perception of what is right, what is wrong, what is good, what is bad, etc. Even though this isn't a bad thing, sometimes it can make us all too critical of ourselves and our lives.

Mindfulness, on the other hand, is the key to self-awareness. It is a specific form of meditation or awareness of the moment. A life lived mindfully affords us a life lived full of peace, tranquility, joy, bliss, ecstasy, and compassion in the midst of challenge, turmoil and the chaos of modern living.

Mindfulness is our direct link to the Universe. It is the solution that we as human beings have been seeking outside ourselves since the beginning of modern times. The simple practice of mindfulness has been around for thousands of years; however, most human beings discard this approach to life and instead search for more complex and intellectual philosophies or techniques.

Chapter 1

You Are The Problem:

Self-Awareness - The First Step Towards Higher Self-Esteem

Self-awareness is the first step towards self-esteem because without knowing who you are you cannot love yourself. It is impossible to love something that you don't know about. The better you know something, the more true love you can give. Self-esteem is essentially built up in three steps: Self-awareness, Self-acceptance, and Self-love. You cannot love yourself if you don't accept yourself and you cannot accept yourself if you are not aware of who you are. Being the first step towards self-esteem, self-awareness is thus extremely important.

Different people get stuck at different stages in this process towards self-esteem. Some people find it extremely difficult to accept themselves and therefore get stuck at the self-acceptance stage. They may not be able to accept their physical appearance, their intelligence level, their emotions or something else about themselves. Because they don't accept all parts of themselves, they can never love themselves to 100%. Other people manage to accept themselves but fail to love themselves. This is usually simply due to a lack of knowledge about how to do it. Once you can accept yourself and know how to turn that acceptance into love, self-esteem comes easily. Many people, however, get stuck because they don't have enough self-awareness. Self-awareness is more than knowing your name, address, shoe size, favorite food, etc. Self-awareness is understanding how you feel and think in different situations and understanding why you feel and think in that way. It's understanding your strengths and weaknesses, it's an ability to listen to yourself and the signs of your body and to use these signs to take care of yourself.

So how do you raise your self-awareness? The only master who can teach you about yourself is you. Therefore, you need to listen to yourself. Listen to your thoughts, listen to your emotions, read your body's signs and observe your actions. Many techniques can help you to do this. Meditation is one of them. This is an ancient technique and modern research has proved that it works. You don't necessarily have to sit in a meditation posture when you meditate. Some people meditate when they are out walking in the forest or when they are lying on the beach. You can also try physical exercises such as yoga or qi gong or other martial arts with a self-focus. If you like writing, there are plenty of writing exercises that raise your self-awareness. Simply keeping a diary helps you to become more self-aware, especially if you go back and re-read what you have written earlier and try to find patterns or developments.

The Missing Link:
Why Self Awareness Is Important in Achieving Success

Whichever way you want to look at it, you will still observe that self-awareness is an essential part of life. Being aware of yourself and the qualities you possess even helps you achieve success. You may be doubtful about that but think about it. How can you expect to achieve your goals when you are not aware of your strengths and weaknesses?

To have more self-awareness will require you to have a more open mind. You may not like certain facts about yourself that you were not even aware of in the first place. One fact that you should be aware of is that you are fascinating. Before you contradict that thought, think about who else is exactly like you. You may share similarities with your parents, but there are no two human beings alike. In learning more about self-awareness, you can take a simple step by asking people how they see you. What do they think are your strengths? What do you think your strengths are as well?

You may be surprised by their replies and what they have to say about you. You will discover that there are many great qualities about you that you were never truly aware of. When you are made more aware of your strengths, you can focus your attention on them. Having more self-awareness is like fitting the pieces of a jigsaw puzzle together. You will begin to understand that there are things and activities that you like and know you will be good at. You can even make an honest assessment of your capabilities and build up your strengths with better choices.

Confidence is what self-awareness brings out and you will surely value yourself even more, especially when you start achieving goals you have set for yourself. Being aware of aspects of your personality can help you find your identity. For example, a strength you always had was a creative mind. You can start developing that creativity and finding ways to let your creative juices flow. You can take up writing or painting and find such an activity to be very stimulating.

There are wonderful benefits to having self-awareness and knowing yourself leads you to make the right choices based on your strengths and abilities. These choices are like the steps that you take towards achieving your goals. As each step is accomplished, you will be even more empowered and feel that you are more than ready to take on any challenge. Of course, nobody likes to have weaknesses, but if you have self-awareness of these, you can work on them.

Being aware of yourself and determining your identity will help you take a more objective approach to view your life and the choices you have made and are planning to make.

Here are different ways of looking at self-awareness. You can take a more philosophical point of view or a more psychological perspective. There are other points of view like leaning more on the theoretical side and even a modern scientific point of view. When self-awareness is achieved by people, it is followed by the setting of standards that are aligned with their core values and strengths. Simply observe people who possess awareness of themselves. Notice how they tackle tasks and accomplish their goals. If you want something like that for yourself, understand what self awareness is and start realizing your potentials today!

Why You Are Not Growing:
Improving Self-Awareness Is Key to Personal Growth

In order to move you first need a destination. In order to grow you need a number of conditions to be met. Just like a plant or an animal, you will fill the space available to you. Place a plant in a small pot and you will effectively stunt its growth. Repot it into a larger pot or plant it outside and suddenly a whole new range of possibilities are created.

You will need some space to grow into, physical space, emotional space, social space, spiritual space, and intellectual space. The challenge for many of us is that we may not even realize that we are in a space that is too small for us.

To be able to do this you will need to have considered your options and goals, challenged the accepted paradigms for you, your family, your culture and perhaps your gender. You need to know who you are, what your goal is in life, your aspirations to discover what makes you unique as a human being, this uniqueness is where your power lies.

Your interactions with peers, colleagues, and friends reflect what kind of person you are. You should be conscious of who you are, how you react to certain situations, especially in dealing with others all without judgment.

Being aware of what you do or how you interact in different circumstances makes you realize that your emotions, habits, values, and personality need to work in conjunction in order to achieve favorable results. When they are on the same wavelength and working together you can make adjustments to deal with every situation you encounter.

These traits, when all are working in unison, become your superpower, revealling the unique way that you'll approach problems, situations, and tasks. We can often try to model our behavior on others when often the best way is to simply be yourself.

It is, therefore, important to understand that improving your self-awareness will lead you to be prepared for further social interactions and later guide your destiny to a happy life. When your values and emotions are working harmoniously, you can make timely interventions to decide which ones should be released and the which ones should be retained.

When everything that you're dealing with, is viewed through the lens of self-awareness you will see that you can measure all of your actions and thoughts to ensure that they are congruent with all your other decisions because you know exactly what you want to come based on your self-assessment. This enables you to be sure that the tasks you would be doing relate to your personal plans. But first, you've got to learn the basics.

1. Know yourself and be willing to make decisions that elicit and not to resist any positive change of yourself.

2. Make it a priority to make yourself fitter in all aspects, e.g. health, mental, spiritual and social endeavors.

3. Study your personality to increase your self-awareness to evaluate your emotions and habits considering which ones can remain, which ones need to be rectified and which ones need to be put into the trash.

4. Reflect all your needs, as Maslow identified them as needs of esteem, affection, belongingness, achievement, self-actualization, power and control. If you understand these needs, this will affect your own behavior and influence your interpersonal relationships with other people. Are you driving or being driven by the most basic of needs?

5. Develop your self-analysis; identify what the positive aspects in your life are that need to be developed and cultivate them to further your aspirations. By focusing on the positives we can ensure that these are the areas that are amplified.

The simple half full vs half empty debate has raged on forever, imagine a new perspective, one of gratitude. If you were thirsty then even a half-empty glass could be a benefit! Without a glass, there would not be a reason to question, similarly without any water and merely a glass there would be even greater cause for alarm. By focusing on the positives will not mean that everything runs smoothly without any roadblocks along the way but you will be able to reframe any obstacles and appreciate them for what they are so that you can move beyond them to realize your dreams.

The Triple Threat:
Integrity, Self-Awareness, and Leadership

Integrity is generally agreed to be a vital quality in a leader. It's usually defined in terms of honesty and adhering strongly to an ethical code. However, when applied to non-human areas such as a body of data, or an ecosystem, something that has 'integrity' is 'intact', 'whole', or 'not tampered with'. This was, in fact, the original meaning of the word (from the Latin meaning 'untouched').

Integrity, therefore, came to mean 'ethically sound' by metaphorical extension. As so often with metaphors applied to human subjective experience, we can discover something useful when we take the metaphor literally.

Consider a person who is grappling with an inner conflict. It may be that two of their most important values are in conflict, or that they cannot choose between alternatives that seem to be equally tempting (or equally scary). Because memory, learning, and behavior are influenced by emotional states, it could even be that what they believe and how they act change significantly depending on how they are feeling.

Can a person who has significant unresolved internal conflicts be a good leader? It's doubtful. Such a person would find it hard to make decisions and stick to them because whichever alternative they choose would leave part of themselves unsatisfied. In addition, when you feel ambivalent about your own decisions, it is hard to defend them against criticism.

So unresolved internal conflicts do not make for good leadership. They lead to indecision, inconsistency, and an inability to stick to your guns - none of which are desirable characteristics in a leader.

To build the sound internal foundation (also known as "character") which is necessary for leadership, you need to identify your values and resolve any values conflicts that you uncover.

Being clear about your values and acting in line with them also means that you will be perceived as "walking your talk" - the key element in leading by example.

The most important thing to remember about emotional intelligence as it applies to leadership is that self-awareness is the foundation on which all the other 'competencies' of emotional intelligence are based. If you are not aware of your own emotions, it's impossible to manage them and hard to understand the emotions of others; in turn, self-management and empathy are prerequisites for being able to handle and inspire emotions in other people.

Leadership takes many forms and can be decoupled from titles and positions quite easily. We all have a responsibility to be a leader, whether that is at home, work, in social settings or somewhere else. We have the opportunity to lead through our consistent action whether we lead a team of 2 or 10,000.

What many people fail to appreciate is that we must lead ourselves daily, our decisions on a minute by minute basis are crucial with regards to our destination. What kind of leader are you in your life?

So far how has your self-leadership style worked out for you? Given your unique mix of skills, challenges, characteristics, and gifts what are your responsibilities?

What leadership decisions have you made so far in your life and what has the impact of those decisions been?

What is your health like today?

How about your financial position?

Have you built the types of relationships you dreamed of?

If your answers to any of these questions leave you feeling down or deflated understand that what we have done is to simply create the **SPACE** we discussed earlier.

This space is for you to grow into, not as healthy as you want to be?

Grow into it.

Not as financially secure as you would have wished at this stage of your life?

Grow into it.

Relationships with those you care about, nothing to celebrate.

Grow into it.

When you appreciate the incredible power that lies in your decisions and how ultimately these decisions set your course it is easier to refuse decisions that give short term rewards and chose decisions that give you what you want in the long term. Some simple examples could include:

You are desperate to improve your health and fitness, after analysis, you realize that you do zero physical activities each week.

First set yourself a fitness target to walk for 10 minutes each day. The next time you are about to jump into your car to get to the local shop, simply ask yourself.

'Is this taking me closer to, or further away from my goals?'

You would like to improve your financial position, after analyzing your income and expenses you realize that you are spending far too much on clothing you never really wear.

First set yourself a monthly saving figure. The next time you are out and you find your self in a buying situation, simply ask yourself.

'Is this taking me closer to, or further away from my goals?'

You want your relationship with your wife to be deeper and more connected, after analysis, you realize that your communication is limited to the organizational side of life.

First, designate a daily time for connection. When something comes up that was not scheduled and you are considering making a call to check if it is okay, simply ask yourself.

'Is this taking me closer to, or further away from my goals?'

Stop Walking Blind:
Recognizing and Obliterating Negative Self-Talk

We often walk blindly, injuring ourselves without necessarily feeling it. By becoming aware of how we communicate with ourselves (sometimes thousands of times per day) we can take the blinkers off, eliminate the silent injuries and begin to thrive.

You can ensure a bright future for yourself if you raise your level of self-awareness. You can enhance your awareness of yourself through self-talk and positive thinking, the keys to a long and successful life.

Living is not fun if you don't have something to look forward to, and goals give you something to work for and something to expect. Setting goals is of great importance in life. And before you can set any goals, you need to enhance your level of self-awareness.

When you become more aware of yourself, you gain more knowledge about yourself. Self-awareness enables an honest and balanced view of your personality, which will, in turn, enable you to interact with your peers confidently and openly.

You can develop self-awareness through positive thinking and self-talk. Simply think positively about your personality and your life. Self-talk, which will help you become more positive in life, is the sure way of gaining self-awareness.

○ Basics of Self-talk

Go to a quiet area in your house or garden. Visualize yourself sitting with another person. You don't have to worry about your safety. The person you are visualizing is your own self. You aim to understand yourself better and the only person you can help you do this is yourself.

Visualize yourself sitting in front of you and communicate with yourself. Ask your self about your feelings, about the things that are going on in your life.

Assure yourself that you are always there for you and that you would always lend yourself a hand.

Encourage yourself so that you can rely on you and give yourself a helping hand whenever you are in need.

The more you get to know yourself, the easier your life is going to be. Don't judge yourself when you engage in self-talk. Instead, make it a fun experience akin to the experience you have when you go out with your friends.

Here is an example to help you get an idea of what happens in self-talk.

Self: How are you?

You: I am fine, but I have been working long hours, and I am really tired.

Self: Why do you work so hard?

You: Well, I have to be loyal to my employer, show dedication toward my work, and deliver prompt results.

Self: What do you get for working so hard?

You: Oh, people show their gratitude sometimes.

Self: How do you feel so?

You: Sometimes, I feel they don't really care.

Self: Ok...

You: Aren't we now thinking out of context?

Self: Not that I know of. We are still traveling in the same vehicle.

You: I am afraid, I am the culprit here. I am thinking about playing golf tonight with the others. I simply don't understand where the thought sprang from.

Self: It came from me; I inspired it. I was just wondering how wonderful it would be to finish work early tonight and just relax and watch a movie instead of hammering away on my keyboard until my fingers ache.

You: That sure sounds like a great idea! I am really feeling extremely stressed. A breath of fresh air is all I need to come back to life after all these long hours of writing.

Self: Well, what stops you from doing just that?

You: Nothing really! Why don't we just go out and have some fun tonight, just you and I?

So, you must have got some idea about self-talk. To a certain extent, all of us indulge in it. Here, you are just doing it consciously.

So, as you see, apart from giving you an enhanced level of self-awareness, self-talk refreshes you and makes you feel more positive toward life.

Challenge

Try this right now, stop reading and spend 3-5 minutes practicing Self-Talk.

Know Yourself:
Six Steps to Self-Awareness

STEP 1: For the next 20 days.

Each day write down one thing you noticed about yourself. If it's an insight all the better, but anything will do and every day doesn't have to be a breakthrough day.

Over time you will compile a substantial body of personal information in your inner work notebook.

Reflect on the fact that your personality must be finite, after all, it lives in the realms of time and space. Every authentic remark and insight into your character is a step toward self-knowledge.

 STEP 2: Watch yourself in social situations, when you're alone, at work, in your primary love relationship and all the other environments, relationships and circumstances in which you act and function. We tend to behave differently according to where we are and who we are with.

Your personality is rich and diverse. There are so many sides to you. Sometimes you forget parts of yourself; sometimes you neglect certain parts and over-indulge others. This exercise will help you to get in touch with all parts of yourself and work toward integration and wholeness.

STEP 3: As human beings, we are always in one of three realms. **Awake**, **Asleep** or **Dreaming**. Now examine each one and study, compare and consider what you can learn about yourself.

Look also at the borders. The borderline between waking and sleeping, for example, is an extraordinarily potent time for accessing the unconscious. Enter into this with the excitement of new adventure and be open to new discoveries.

STEP 4: Self-observation is far harder than observing others, probably because it's less challenging than observing ourselves and because we have become predominantly visual in our experience of the world. But this doesn't mean that observing others is necessarily unhelpful to your inner work practice.

So, observe others. Choose someone at a party, in the street or at work and see how much you can learn about them through witnessing their body posture, their speed, their tone of voice, walking gait, functionality, general attitude. Do they speak using visual imagery, mental abstractions or touchy-feely terminology? This will tell you a great deal about them. How do they react with others? Privately compile a set of information, a profile of them, until you have insights that are way beyond a glancing acquaintanceship. Now, the testing time: can you do the same with yourself?

STEP 5: Background assumptions and wallpaper beliefs are your moral suppositions, guiding principles and taken-for-granted expectations. They are like the water we swim in or the air we breathe.

Make them conscious. They were communicated to you by parents, teachers and authority figures in domestic, educational and societal settings in your early life. They dictate your attitude to time, money, love, ambition, action, relationships, success, failure, and happiness. Bringing them to conscious awareness over time allows you to reconsider and make new empowered choices.

 STEP 6: What do you do? What do you want? What is your life purpose? For many of us, there is a disparity between these three aspects of life. Can you see that when they are in alignment and correct proportion to each other, balance and success must surely ensue?

Make a chart: list your actions - working, relaxing, watching TV, reading, spending time with your family. List your needs and desires - I want to make money (how much?), I want to create a loving family environment, I want to learn to play a musical instrument. Finally, write down or explore your life purpose.

Now, as you do this you will start to notice discrepancies; things you want that you don't allow yourself the time for, doing too much of this and not enough of that, procrastination and unreal expectations. Once you get the full picture, you may want to change it.

Chapter 2

What is Mindfulness?

Mindfulness is the act of bringing your awareness to whatever you're experiencing in the present moment. A common definition of mindfulness used in counseling and therapy is; The awareness that emerges through paying attention on purpose, in the present moment, and non-judgementally to things as they are.

When we don't pay attention to the present moment, we go through life relatively absentmindedly, often distracted and on auto-pilot. We've all encountered moments of "mindlessness" when, instead of paying attention to what we are doing, our minds are off somewhere else: daydreaming, dwelling on the past, worrying about the future, or juggling so many things at once that our mind is all over the place.

Mindfulness is the opposite of mindlessness. Mindfulness involves paying attention to whatever we are doing while we are doing it, and whatever we are experiencing while we are experiencing it. We acknowledge whatever is going on in our lives, in the outside world and our inner experience, as it is happening.

When we practice mindfulness, we learn to deal with whatever is going on in our lives, and with our thoughts and emotions, without becoming overwhelmed. By paying attention to our experience from moment to moment we can start fully living our lives in the present, instead of functioning automatically and unconsciously, getting lost in our thoughts, or escaping into memories of the past or plans for the future.

Mindfulness meditation is one way to practice mindfulness, but since mindfulness simply involves paying attention to the present moment, mindfulness can be brought to anything you do. You can become more mindful without meditation, and even if you do practice mindfulness meditation, the benefits of mindfulness are greatest when mindfulness is incorporated into everyday life. Many of my clients never practice meditation and find other ways to bring mindfulness into their lives.

How to Expand Your Mind For Success

Reading, writing and tasking your mind to supply answers to tough questions, are some of the ways of exercising it. It is a known fact that physical exercise and eating healthy foods keep your body fit and strong. Likewise, reading books, formal education, parental guidance, street education and mentoring expands your mind for success.

Some of the factors capable of expanding the mind are as follows;

o   Books

Read books in various subjects. Study the dictionary, magazines, newspapers, religious books, self-help books, autobiographies, biographies and historical books. Surf the internet which is the biggest library in the world to read, Wikipedia, personal development articles in websites and blogs, to fill your mind with information and become knowledgeable.

Reading all kinds of literature in diverse media would fill your mind with general and unique information in different fields of human endeavor. As you continue with this habit, the knowledge you have gathered elevates your thought creating patterns of order, so that retrieving information to solve problems when confronted with one becomes easy. To become useful to yourself, your local community and the world, read diverse materials to enrich your store of knowledge to expand your mind to meet needs and become a global problem solver.

o   Formal Education

Formal education is learning which you go through from early childhood to young adulthood. In many countries across the world, it is your fundamental human right to have formal education. It is highly recommended that you get at least the first 12 years of formal education. During this period, your mind expands by the knowledge you acquire from reading and teachers lectures.

Formal education gives you basic preparation for life's challenges. Some people pass through elementary school to high school and then to college. Whereas for others, their formal training stops at high school and street education takes over till they become streetwise. Formal education prepares you for a particular occupation. But the training is usually incomplete hence you must add experience to it, to sharpen your mind.

As you solve one problem after another, maturity comes naturally and you become better as time passes. Though formal education enriches the mind, by far the greatest teacher is the problems you solve as each day passes. The tougher it is, the harder you have to dig into your mind to fetch answers. The key to expanding your mind lay in stretching your imagination and believing in your ability to solve whatever problems or tasks you meet.

o   Parental Guidance

Your parents are your first teachers. You learned most of what you know from early childhood to adolescent, from them. Active parental guidance and education continue until you leave home. Your parents teach you good morals; help you find your natural talent, teach you to set goals. Their mentoring impacts you so much you innocently copy some of their habits (either good or bad). They teach you to love your country, your duties and responsibilities as a citizen, poise, and self-esteem, having healthy relationships and being a good person to live a fruitful life and to serve your God. All you learned at home, formed part of the pool of information in your brain for use to solve problems. Consequently, parental mentoring is important to your life and your hope of living a life of abundance. It is during your stay with your parents that you form most of your beliefs and mindsets on issues; hence their role is invaluable as major players in helping you expand your mind.

o   Street Education

You get street education in the cold hard streets. The challenges and circumstances you face in the streets toughen you to act in a certain way. When you become grounded in the unwritten rules of survival in the streets, you become streetwise and no one could easily take advantage of you. As time goes on, exposure to dangerous street laws and ways enables you to mature quickly in the affairs of life. During this time of growth, your sixth sense kicks in to detect any scam when you see one and meet difficulties head-on without backing-down prematurely.

Street education in addition to information gathered through experience expands your mind. Use it to make decisions in a flash. For example, when you face danger and the situation requires split seconds decisions and where failure to decide could mean life or death, your mind rises to the occasion because it has material to work with after several years of street education.

In the streets, you learn self-preservation and to execute tasks speedily. In the streets, it is survival of the fittest, and you are strictly on your own, trusting no one and taking no prisoners. As you go through tough training in the streets, your mind expands so fast and continues to develop as you face one hard situation after another and conquer them all.

o Mentoring

Mentoring grants you unique access to the resources of your mentor. When you learn from role models, it saves you years you would have toiled using trial and error methods.

Mentoring enables you to learn the intricacies of your mentor's field of expertise. Mentoring expands your mind as the mentor's abilities, knowledge, and expertise are gradually transferred to your mind. Mentoring accelerates your mental development so much. You copy and execute mind growth strategies and apply them quickly to your life and circumstances.

The information you gather through this method helps you to expand in the specific field, business, or service you receive mentoring for. Mentoring also adds to the collection of information and knowledge you gather and store in your mind like a computer database, which you retrieved when the need arose.

In addition to being mentored, there is another level that holds even greater rewards. Becoming a mentor for someone. Being an advocate for someone and sometimes simply dreaming for them until they arrive at a place where they can dream for themselves is a _____.

Who can you ask to be your mentor or who can you mentor today?

o   Experience

Experience teaches you hard lessons in life. What you go through as you grow up, are usually deeply engraved in your mind. Your experience could be either good or bad, but this does not matter. Either way, experience helps to shape how you respond to challenges in life.

For instance, your experience in a job gives you competence and excellent abilities. It could also guide you when setting up a business, choosing the type of business to set up the decisions and actions you take to run that business. As you face different tough situations daily, you grow up physically and developed mentally because your mind is continually being expanded by what you believe is possible or not. Please note that it is the level of wisdom and its application in your life determines your growth, and not your content or context.

What you say is possible remains possible. You are only limited by what you believe. You must realize that facts and knowledge you have stored in your mind, influence your belief system. So to make experience pay great dividends to expand your mind daily, and apply superior insights to solve difficult problems.

Conclusively, in life, no knowledge is a waste. All the information you gather is important for molding you into the kind of person you grow up to become. In this information age, things change rapidly hence, you must become very knowledgeable and smart if you are aspiring for the top twenty percent of those making an impact in the world. From the foregoing, to expand your mind is no longer a choice but a necessity for success.

Make efforts to acquire more information on a daily basis to expand your mind and enable you to become more productive, confident and successful. An expanded mind is like a garden full of choice flowers. With an expanded mind, you always have abundant choices and strategies to tackle challenges life throws at you.

Mindfulness Meditation

Mindfulness meditation is often confused with other forms of meditation. The main target when concentrating is to try and focus on a particular part of the body or the mind, to reach a target and develop a certain ability.

Activities like "Thai-chi" and "Yoga", are both forms of concentration. Mindfulness meditation, however, is different, its purpose is to completely free the mind of any thoughts, relaxing the body to such an extent that every thought disappear. This state can last anything from a few seconds to many hours depending on your ability. To reach the highness of spirituality, you must reach the highness of purity in your mind.

To reach this state you must concentrate on the "sound within yourself" to reach the "light within yourself". A place far away at the end of a long and dark place. The light is getting closer and closer and when we reach the end of the tunnel and embrace the light, the blessing that we receive cannot be explained. To reach this state we have to reach a pure state through Mindfulness meditation, have "pure" intention and concentrate on the "sound" of the inner you.

Mindfulness meditation seems like it's giving us the means to reach a mental purity, and there are several techniques that one can use to meditate effectively, many of them utilize the Mantra, which is a collection of words and sounds that get repeated mentally to help us reach our target. Mantra is sacred, there are many ways to apply the mantra, and no mantra is better than the other, and it is extremely important to reach that state of purity of the mind.

1- Mantra is a very simple thought, and it becomes more natural and familiar, as we repeat in our minds. This thought is used to substitute all of our other thoughts, and every time a different thought comes into our head we substitute it with the mantra.

2- When we exercise in the mindful meditation that uses the Mantra, we tend to associate the mantra to a condition of calmness. This association is called Neuro-Linguistic Programming. After having trained for this, even if we are tense about something, thinking about the mantra will immediately take us to a condition of calmness. This makes the Mantra an indispensable tool that we can use to face the most stressful situations that we have in the course of our life.

When we understand the Mantra, and how it works it becomes very evident that changing techniques in which the Mantra is applied is not always a good thing to do. Changing Mantra is good only in special situations when we need to eliminate a habit that is impeding us to reach a certain mental condition. It is also obvious the Mantra that we use should be reserved to ourselves if we disclose this information we give other the chance to control our mind. The best mindful meditation teachers will abstain from giving away the best mantras available and concentrate only on one.

Mantra is usually made of a vowel alternated to some nasal sounds and it can contain several words. The most famous mantra is "oooooh" or "aaaaummm", but any other word can do the same job if we extend the vowel and the nasal sound. it is better if the mantra contains a spiritual word, a word which means a gift to God rather than a commonly used word that has no affinity to the spiritual world. Who does not wish to sing religious chants, could alternatively use other unusual words to obtain the same result. Mantra literally means Manas = Mind, and Trya = To Free Both together forms the sentence '**Free your mind**'.

The position assumed during meditation is extremely important, the easiest position is a comfortable one with your spine straight, too much relaxation and you will probably fall asleep. Join your hands and stretch your legs to create a Bio-energy field around you. The typical Yoga position is another good one, but it needs a certain dexterity or the fetus position.

If you have never tried mindfulness meditation, find a quiet place and try the following technique:

1- Assume one of the positions mentioned earlier, it has to be a comfortable one to meditate effectively.

2- Close your eyes and relax every muscle in your body including your face. Breathe and exhale alternatively from one nostril only. Close a nostril each time with your finger while alternating breaths.

3- Try to ignore every thought that comes into your head, trying to create a space in your head. If a thought comes into your mind try to use a mental Mantra like " oooohhhmmmm " to eliminate it. You can carry on counting and eliminating thoughts without analyzing them and when you are down to 2 or 3 thoughts in the space of five minutes it means you are meditating effectively.

With a little practice, you should be able to achieve the freedom of the mind through mindfulness meditation in every place, even if full of people utilizing the technique of the Mantra. Use the Mantra regularly until you have enough meditation experience as the thought of the Mantra is associated with a free mind.

One of the benefits of mindfulness meditation is that it opens your mind to new ideas, become more creative or solves your problems. Try to think of your mind as a glass full of water, if you put more water it will just spill out. Many intelligent people do meditate regularly, Albert Einstein and Edison notoriously meditated in different forms throughout the years.

Mindfulness Meditation to Suppress Anxiety

Many studies have recently shown, much to the delight of the yoga community, that mindfulness meditation is scientifically verified to help reduce anxiety. It is sometimes called mindfulness-based stress reduction, or **MBSR** when studied in a scientific setting, but it is a mindful form of meditation through and through. These studies show particular promise for mindfulness meditation in the treatment of Social Anxiety Disorder, or SAD, and in combination with cognitive-behavioral therapy. Hybrids between cognitive behavioral therapy and mindfulness meditation have even been developed, called mindfulness-based cognitive therapy. Participants who undergo mindfulness-based cognitive therapy are found to have a reduction not only in anxiety symptoms but also in depression symptoms.

Research into the effect of meditation on social anxiety has revealed a mindful form of meditation can change the self-image of participants. In one study headed by psychology researcher Philippe Goldin, participants meditated and then were told to select adjectives that described them. After meditation, they were more likely to select adjectives such as "admired" or "loved" but less likely to pick adjectives such as "coward" or "afraid." Participants showed favor toward all positive words after meditation. This suggests a mindful meditation bestows a feeling of well being on the practitioner, with radical psychological consequences, rather than simply raising awareness or giving the practitioner more tools.

The effect of self-knowledge and awareness certainly shouldn't be underestimated either. Long touted as the primary psychological benefit of being mindful during meditation, it has far-reaching consequences, particularly for social anxiety sufferers. Since anxiety is formed from negative emotions in the past and unhelpful projections into the future, bringing awareness to the moment cuts off the main mechanism of social anxiety, and indeed anxiety in general. Those who practice mindfulness meditation learn to see their thoughts for what they are, simply thoughts and not necessarily truths. This helps anxiety sufferers detach from the spiral of negative thoughts that so often causes anxiety, freeing their emotions to respond to other things. Eventually, this can stop the habitual cycle of self-defeating thoughts altogether.

To practice, mindfulness meditation only takes ten minutes out of your day. Some meditate for longer periods, and some meditate for shorter periods, but ten minutes is the recommended time to help with psychological issues. Simply find a quiet place to sit or lie down, and close your eyes. Concentrate on each breath. Thoughts will arise; simply observe them. With continued practice, you'll learn much about yourself and improve your quality of life.

Mindfulness Exercises
The Practise of Being Aware

There are a wide range of ways of practicing mindfulness and I will share some of these mindfulness exercises with you, but the key thing I want you to take on board is to just do it - and keep doing it! Your mind (and your ego) will resist and you will want to become more informed about it and will want to read yet another book about mindfulness.

The human mind loves to make this simple thing so complicated - yet mindfulness is called a practice for a good reason!

Your mind will get bored and want to be entertained, distracted and engaged. That's what minds do, and that's why they are sometimes referred to as "monkey minds". If you want to learn mindfulness exercises - just be mindful - focus your attention, focus your mind, 100% on whatever it is that you are doing right now - in this present moment.

Mindfulness exercises can be divided into:

o   Activity-based exercises and observational exercises

Both types of exercise can be undertaken in groups or on your own.

Typical activity-based mindfulness practices include:

✓ Walking
✓ Physical exercises e.g. Tai Chi
✓ Eating
✓ Undertaking routine household/domestic chores

- ✓ Undertaking outdoor tasks e.g. gardening, clearing land, raising crops

Typical observational mindfulness exercises include:

- ✓ Breathing
- ✓ Body awareness and deep relaxation
- ✓ Sitting meditation
- ✓ Mindful silence
- ✓ Mindful listening
- ✓ Putting it into practice

In my own experience, there is a great benefit in undertaking some of these mindfulness exercises with other people who are doing the same practice. This might be just one other person or as part of a wider practice group.

There is a stronger energy to the activity if is undertaken with others and this can be very encouraging and helpful in your practice of mindfulness.

However, the real work is done on your own and this largely falls into two categories:

(1) Formal practice - this is where you apply regular focused attention to one or two mindfulness exercises at a time, until you have mastered them, and they have become habits. As with the acquisition of any new skill, this requires self-discipline, persistence, and consistency:

"Just be mindful - focus your attention, focus your mind, 100% on whatever it is that you are doing right now - in this present moment."

(2) Integration practice- this is when you take your newly acquired mindfulness skills and apply them at different times of the day.

This may be a "situation-specific" practice when for example you get into a frequently occurring situation such as heavy traffic, or an interaction with a partner or work colleague who irritates you.

Applying mindfulness in relationship situations can be very instructive and very powerful, and over time can change negative and destructive aspects of some relationships.

Mindfulness and Intimacy:
Gaining Self-Awareness, Personal Growth and a Successful Relationship

Mindfulness means, that you pay attention to and are aware of whatever happens within you, regarding your life and relationships. When you practice mindfulness you become empowered to develop a successful and healthy intimacy.

The reason being, that the more you pay attention the more aware you become of yourself (your needs, fears, expectations, fantasies, reactions, and behaviors); as you become aware of yourself the more empowered you become to make conscious decisions regarding your life and relationships (whether you currently have a relationship or attempt to develop one).

Four layers of a mindfulness intimacy are:

1. Paying attention, which enables you to stop acting on automatic pilot. As you pay attention you become able to act with full awareness, making appropriate decisions regarding situations you encounter in your life and your relationships (either with your current partner or with a new partner). When you pay attention, notice and become aware of what there is, you can then decide what changes you would like to make.

2. Observation: Paying attention is based on observation: you observe yourself, your thoughts, attitudes and emotions, reactions and behaviors.

3. Acceptance: when you observe, with full mindfulness and pay attention to what is, you must accept what you notice. Acceptance is vital, since as long as you don't accept what there is you can't make a change, because whilst you deny what is there you will not see a need for change.

4. Making a change: Change is only possible when you accept what you observe. Denying and rejecting what you see won't lead you to personal growth (and to living life and relationships to the fullest, since you don't accept parts of yourself which are, after all, parts of "who you are", parts which often lead you to harm your relationships).

When you observe, pay attention and accept, you can then make a change. The reason being, that you become free to make conscious decisions, rather than continue acting on automatic pilot (like you might have acted until now). Being free you can contemplate new ways of behavior (rather than behaving, once again, according to your old harmful patterns), choosing a behavior that you think/feel best suits you and the current situation, whether with your current partner or in a new relationship.

Be careful not to be your own worst enemy

There are those whom the process of mindfulness might scare them, who might prefer to go on with things as they are rather than look inwards and make changes. If you are among them, you might **deny** and **reject**, rather than **accept** what you **observe**. You will then convince yourself that you don't have such attitudes, behaviors and/or characteristics; that you are not responsible for whatever it is that goes wrong with your relationship. You will also convince yourself that you know yourself well enough and that there is nothing you need to explore and learn about yourself.

Such self-conviction might misguide you: it will "persuade" you that you are o.k. (and your partner not); that you know yourself well enough (even if you don't); that there is nothing for you to change (even if there is).

If you take the "easy route" - accepting these convictions rather than beginning with the process of mindfulness. paying attention, observing, becoming aware and accepting what you see - you sabotage yourself, by not enabling yourself to see things you need to see (about yourself, your partner and your relationship) and making the decisions you need to make in order to finally become empowered to develop a successful, healthy and satisfying intimate relationship.

How to benefit from the process of mindfulness

When you get up the courage and the motivation to go through the process of mindfulness, observe, pay attention, become aware and accept what you see, the more self-understanding and personal-growth you'll gain, and the more empowered you become to develop a successful intimate relationship.

Using Mindfulness for Business Success

If you are in business you have a lot of stress and this can make it difficult to make the right business decisions. There's so much going on that you might not be in the moment when you need to divert your attention to something. In essence, you're not being mindful of the current situation and this can cost you business deals or bring other hardships to your business. To be successful in business you need to be mindful of your current surroundings and situation. Let see how this works and how you can apply it to your own business.

The Act of Thinking Now

Imagined you have a busy day at the office and you have things to do but you're thinking about a big upcoming business meeting. You are so focused on that meeting that you can't get anything done. This lack of focus now puts you behind and you have to struggle in the coming days to catch up. This further increases your stress levels about the big meeting and when the meeting finally arrives you're so stressed out that it's a big failure.

In business, we have to focus on what we can do today and not so much on what we can do tomorrow. You can focus on tomorrow when that day comes. If you focus your mind now, you'll get more done during the day. Our brains can only process so much information in the day and of you overload yourself with other thoughts then the tasks of the day just won't get done. You need to be mindful of the present and work in the present, not the future which is coming up. The time to think about the future is when it arrives as you can deal with it then when your mind is fresh and focused on that problem at that time period.

Worry About the Now which You Can Change

The future isn't something you can change because it hasn't arrived yet. We don't know what we are going to do tomorrow let alone three weeks from now. You have to focus your mind on things that you can change today as this is where you need the most focus in your business. This isn't to say you can't think about the future or where you want to be in the future but by making a decision today you will help that future along. The changes that you make today will impact the future so concentrate on what you can do today and not so much what you can or cannot do tomorrow. This is the approach of the most successful entrepreneurs.

It Takes Time to Be Mindful

It can take time to be mindful so don't try to do it all at once. If you're at a meeting for example, during the day; try to focus all your energy at that one meeting.

Forget about the rest of the day or what you're doing after work and just focus on that one event. This will make it easier to train your mind to find the clarity it needs to concentrate on just one thing in that one moment when you need all your energy.

This is a key to business success. If you can focus on just one thing this can actually reduce your stress too because your mind isn't going in a million different directions and you'll also make better businesses decisions as a result of being more mindful of the present moment and not the future even if that future is just a few hours away.

Conclusion

So we've shared so much valuable information, insights, and wisdom. In order to Stop Losing though, we can't afford to sit on the knowledge that has the power to change our lives! It's time to act, take charge, and win in every area of life that you will. Now that is true power, and it's in your hands.

The goal of self-awareness and mindfulness is to help you recognize the person you are so as to lead yourself in the direction of positive change. Help yourself become the best you can be and find joy in every step you take in that direction. Stop losing today and become a winner in all that you do, not by chance or luck, rather by design. Moving forward keep this question in your back pocket always accessible and ready to pose.

'Is this taking me closer to, or further away from my goals?'

Finally somewhere in this book I have chosen to omit a word. If you have been truly mindful whilst reading you will have noticed this. If you have found it email, authoranthonyodle@gmail.com with your suggestion for the word that should be placed in the void. I look forward to your suggestions.

ACKNOWLEDGEMENTS

This book is dedicated to my Grandfather Arthur James Lawrence.

For the unabated hope and joy, you spread, for reminding me that the setbacks in life often slow us down just enough for us to appreciate the sights along the way. For the example you set and the legacy you left behind.

Finally I would like to thank God, for the blessings and gifts to seize this opportunity to share beyond my circle. To create a tool that can be used by others to create space to grow into who they are designed to be.

Ex Nihilo

ABOUT THE AUTHOR

Anthony Odle is an Author, Educator, Public Speaker and Performance Coach and has been teaching design for over 20 years. Everything he does centers around empowering others. He has taught thousands of young people and hundreds of adults to reframe their 'perception of self' in order to achieve their specific goals, whether academic, business-related or personal fitness goals.

Stop Losing: Master The Art of Self Awareness and Mindfulness is his first book and draws upon his vast experience dealing with and helping others to solve problems to do with self.

Hapilly married for 21 years and the proud father of 5, people generally ask him "where does he find the time and energy to do all of the things that he does" to which he responds "within". He enjoys spending time with the family, working out, watching action movies, and playing video games. He offers online high-performance coaching for those who want to **Stop Losing** and reach their full potential.

AFTERWORD

Anthony is the founder of Vanquish All Enemies a Strength and Conditioning company for the everyday athlete (people who want to be leaner, faster, stronger and fitter) that provides online fitness programmes that incorporate what he considers to be the missing ingredient which is, Mindset Development to ensure that results can be maintained.

"Most people fail because of their mindset. strengthen yours as you strengthen your body".

http://www.instagram.com/vanquishallenemies

He is also a co-founder of Paradigm Pure Health, an optimised wellness company that specialises in identifying the root causes that imbalance body, mind and relationships. Once our clients know better they can choose to do better utilising the best non invasive technology in combination with the power of nature to find out more about improving Physical wellness with bio-scans, visit

https://paradigmpurehealth.com/health-scanning

Printed in Great Britain
by Amazon

31214683R00030